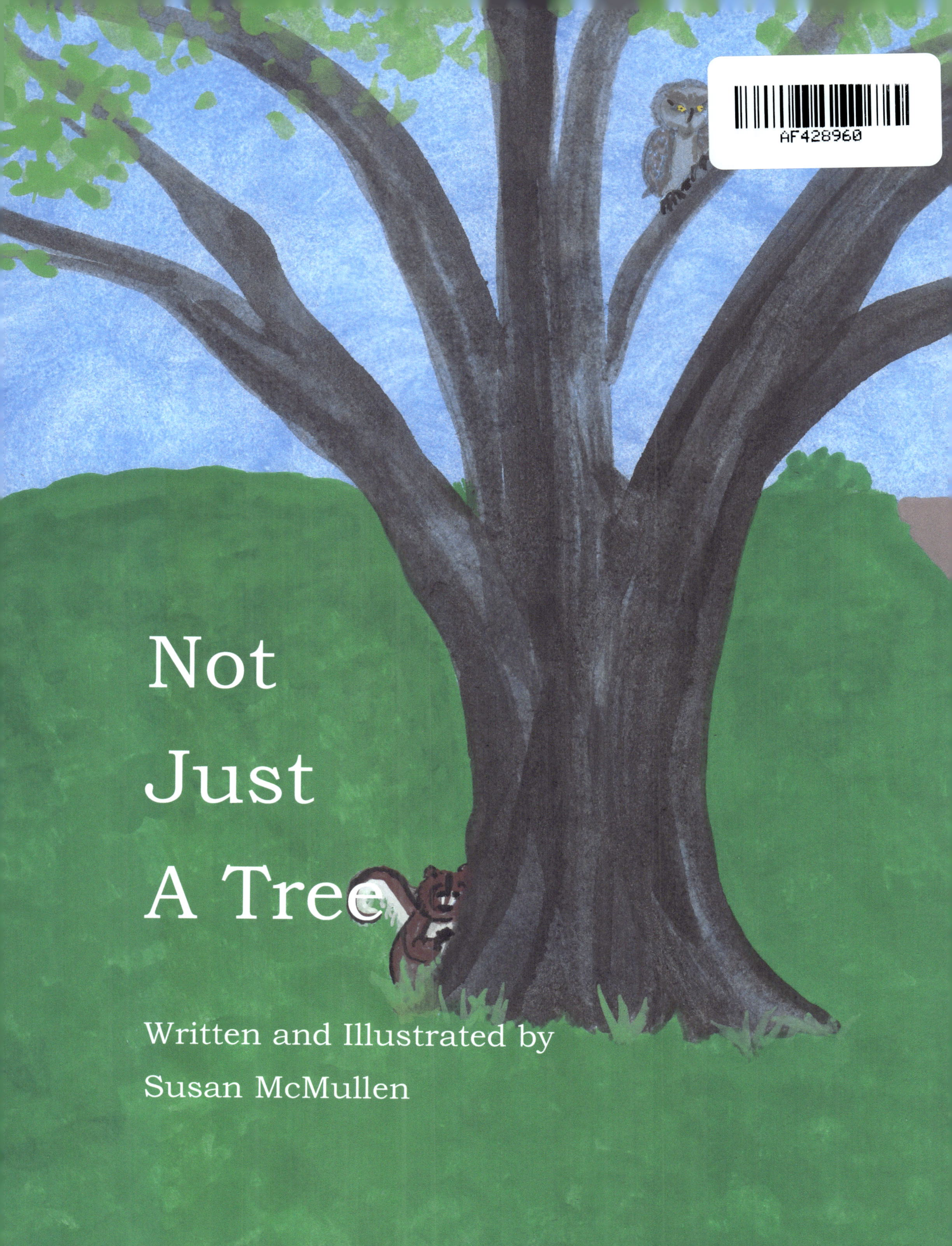

Not
Just
A Tree

Written and Illustrated by
Susan McMullen

Dedicated to my husband, David,

who is my rock and soft spot to land,

and to my children,

David and Hannah,

who are my heart

and the hope I see in the world.

Where would I be

without all your love and support?

I thank God you are part of my life.

There once was a tiny seed
that blew north in the wind
from its mother tree.

It landed in warm, nurturing soil and grew to be a strong, sturdy tree.

It was not a tall tree but a tree
with lots of reaching branches.

As it grew, the tree waved as walkers passed by and swayed with them as they stopped to listen to the musical breeze made by the leaves of the tree.

When the tree was fully
grown and its leaves lush,
it shaded the ones who came to sit
amongst her branches.

Shining rays of sunlight and love,
its sprawling branches reached down
enveloping and comforting
the visitors.

The tree loved to make music
for people and animals alike.

Many small creatures
called it home and used
it as shelter, even people.

One day, a person decided that they
wanted a piece of the pretty tree
and cut off one of its limbs,
leaving the tree hurt
and out of balance.

Its music changed, and her
shade was not quite the same

However,
the tree overcame the cut
and continued to grow and care
for those who came to live
and visit, giving shade
and shelter.

On another day,
a man came to see the tree who
wanted only to leave his mark
on the tree,
so he cut his initials
into her trunk.

The tree wept
for days but
healed and continued to feel
the changing
seasons of the year.

The tree grew and weathered
through the sprouting of spring,

through the chill of winter,

through the heat of summer,

and the beauty of fall.

But still, people kept
leaving their mark on the tree, taking
pieces for their own use, and the tree
dwindled.
It did not thrive as it used to,
shriveling instead of
shimmering,
creaking instead of singing …
just surviving.

One day, a man who knew about trees came and thought he could help the tree.

He first put a sign beside the tree
asking visitors not to harm the tree.
It needed to be nurtured
with kindness and care
to recover from its sickly state.

Several seasons went by.
The man watered, fed, and pruned the
tree.

Soon, the tree was
starting to mend and
strengthen again.

One beautiful spring
day, bright new leaves
began to sprout. They
glistened in the sun,
and the man knew that
there was hope for the
tree.

Once again, the tree began
to give comfort and shade to its many
visitors, human and animal alike.

From the author ...

Just like the tree, people get hurt by other people. However, like the tree you can grow and gain strength from what caused you pain. Even if you have been hurt physically or emotionally, you can continue to shine! Do not hide your light under a bushel because of someone else! Shine and shimmer like the leaves of the pretty tree.

Help keep the Earth clean and healthy. Please recycle, reuse, and repurpose.

We all share the same air and water.

We need trees to breathe and water to live.

Take pictures, bring what you love ... but leave only footprints.

About the author ...

I am a native of Florida and have lived in the Tallahassee area since I was adopted at the age of 3 weeks. I am a graduate of Florida State University and a current employee. In fact, I have roamed the campus of FSU since I was 4 years old and attended my first football game, along with being a graduate of their K-12 school, Florida High.

I am married and have two children, who currently are in their twenties. Not only are we family, the four of us are also friends. Our children are spreading their wings in different regions of the country and my husband and I spend as much time in nature as we can. I also love to create art in all kinds of ways.

In the past, I have worked as a cashier, stockperson, free lance artist, handyman, housekeeper, reading tutor, bank teller, caterer, cake designer and classroom teacher. I consider myself an educator, I love learning and feel that you should learn something new every day! Currently, I educate in a different way working with college students, about life skills. I have experienced many things in my 53 years of life and have always tried to spread positive seeds, hoping for positivity to spread. Life is full of hard lessons. We must weather the storm and learn from them.

I hope my story helps another weather the storms life brings us from time to time.